Minding my Keys and Pews

My Life as a Part-Time Organist

JOANNA ADICKS WALLACE

Minding My Keys and Pews: My Life as a Part-Time Organist
by Joanna Adicks Wallace

copyright ©2016 Joanna Adicks Wallace

Trade paperback ISBN: 978-1-943294-43-5
Ebook ISBN: 978-1-943294-44-2

Cover design by Martijn van Tilborgh

Published by Kudu Publishing

Minding My Keys and Pews is also available on Amazon Kindle, Barnes & Noble Nook and Apple iBooks.

Contents

Dedication...5

Acknowledgements...7

Part I: How Firm a Foundation
1. In the Beginning...11
2. The Solid Rock...15
3. Practice Plus..17
4. Faux Pas..23

Part II: The Family of God
5. Organ Committees...27
6. The Honeymoon Period.................................31
7. The Nuts and Bolts of the Job........................33
8. Balancing Act..35
9. Traditional or Contemporary?.......................37
10. Dante Who?...39
11. Church Life and Relationships.....................41
12. Surely the Presence.....................................43

Part III: Count Your Blessings
13. Family Ties..47
14. Our Professional Organization.....................51

Part IV: The Bond of Love
15. Easy Money?..59

16 Counting the Cost 61

17. The Perfect Wedding Pastor 65

18. Language Barrier... 67

19. Wedding Consultants I Have Known 69

20. Fascinating Grooms...................................... 73

21. Fiascoes and Other Fun 75

Part V: He Giveth More Grace

22. Beyond the Sanctuary................................. 81

23. The Substitute Organist 83

24. Unexpected Happenings at the Keyboard.................. 89

Part VI: Turn Your Eyes Upon Jesus

25. Poise Is Everything 99

26. When in Our Music God Is Glorified...................... 101

Dedication

I dedicate this book to the memory of my brother, Dr. Richard R. Adicks, Jr., who autographed my copy of his book: "Now it's your turn."

Acknowledgements

SPECIAL THANKS GO OUT to my friends and fellow authors at Word Weavers Orlando. Your thoughtful (and sweetly stated) critiques have been a blessing to me. You kept me inspired to finish what I started.

Much love and appreciation to Alicia Pagán, Sra. Nilda Rosa, and Fundacion Belen Figueroa, Inc. for their prayers, love, support, and encouragement in seeing that this book is produced as God would have it.

My grateful appreciation to my wonderful editor, mentor, and friend, Marti Picper, who has blessed me greatly with her God-given skills as we worked together on the book.

My thanks to the brilliant John Leatherman for his suggested title.

My gratitude to Diana Scimone for her seminar on "How to Write a Book" so long ago when she asked us to jot down everything about a favorite subject. How startling to hear you say, "There's your book."

To my husband, Hugh, thank you for patiently waiting for this to happen and for encouraging me to write—for your love and constant support of all my artistic endeavors.

I. HOW FIRM A FOUNDATION:
MY EARLY DAYS WITH THE ORGAN

CHAPTER 1

In the Beginning

I HAVE ALWAYS LOVED MUSIC. When I was a little girl in Lake City, Florida, our family piano fascinated me. Mother would sit down at that old Cable upright and play so we could sing along. Whenever we traveled to Jacksonville, the "big city," we always went to a huge department store where Mother would buy popular sheet music. I loved watching the people who played piano there as they worked inside a big rectangle of racks filled with sheet music. Mother chose a piece of music and handed it to one of the clerks, who sat down and played it for her.

I decided that my ambition in life was to be one of those musicians at the department store—the best job in the whole world. I imagined the excitement of spending my life playing the piano. When we brought the sheet music home, we could hardly wait for Mother to go over all of the songs. We stood behind her and sang the pop tunes of the day.

As a six-year-old in first grade, I watched my older brother play his simple first-year pieces. Sitting on the bench, I pushed him over so I could play those notes. I couldn't read them, but I looked at the fingering numbers and played his music. He complained to Mother, "Joanna pushed me off the bench again."

Mother went to his music teacher and said, "I don't know what to do. Joanna keeps pushing Richard off the bench."

Miss Porter suggested that I take lessons, too. "I don't usually take a student until they've finished first grade," she said. "She'll either take to it or get bored and leave him alone."

My proud mother reported that, a few months later, my teacher told her, "It would have been a shame not to give Joanna piano lessons." And so began my love of the keyboard as well as my lifelong career.

During my fourth-grade year, Miss Porter taught lessons in our school's old brown wooden building. My classroom was at the other end of the second-floor hallway. I walked on those creaky floors down the hall to her room after school once a week for my lesson. One day she told me she wanted me to present a mini-concert for my classmates. Having to sing "I'm Called Little Buttercup" was embarrassing, but fortunately the rest of the recital was piano pieces, which I enjoyed playing.

By that time, I had begun playing complex classical compositions. One big occasion took place when I was in fifth grade. I was invited to play a piano number over in the high school building for the students' Wednesday-morning assembly.

By the time I was twelve years old, I played songs and hymns for Sunday school classes at our church, First Presbyterian in Lake City, Florida. The children loved the lively way I played the wonderful Fanny Crosby hymn "Praise Him! Praise Him!" One summer when I was in high school, I went each Sunday to nearby White Springs with an elder who preached at a small church. I played as the congregation sang hymns.

During one period in my high school years, I found myself too busy with many organizations and school projects, so I slacked off in practicing. On lesson days, I gulped down my supper and ran to the piano to grab a few minutes, trying to make up for a week with no practice at all. Then I raced to the car to drive to Miss Porter's. I would arrive about fifteen or twenty minutes late for my thirty-minute lesson.

My teacher would often let me have my thirty minutes, listening to me practice a new piece for the first time while the next student waited on the porch in one of her rocking chairs. Such a patient lady! Once in a while, she would be firm and tell me she only had ten minutes left to teach me that evening. That cured my tardiness for a week or two.

My mother once more had a down-to-earth conversation with my teacher. Miss Porter said, "Keep her coming to lessons. After a while, she'll decide to get back to practicing." Bless her heart. She was such a wise and dear little spinster lady who was correct as usual.

Years later, I studied organ at the University of Florida. My organ professor, the university organist, Claude Murphree, once came to Lake City for an event. I introduced him to Miss Porter and he said, "I am so glad to get to meet Joanna's wonderful piano teacher."

What a blessing for her to hear that! She deserved many accolades just for surviving her time with me.

My mother and Miss Mary Porter brought me a life filled with music. I am a wife and mother and have also been a teacher and secretary. But having music as a side career has both inspired me and brought me an additional income. I'm so thankful for my heritage of music.

CHAPTER 2

The Solid Rock

L ITTLE OF WHAT WE DO as organists amounts to much unless we have a foundation for our efforts. The rock we Christian organists rely on is Jesus Christ, our Savior, mentor, guide, and friend. If it had not been for Him and the salvation He offers, I would never have been guided into my chosen field.

I received Jesus as my Lord and Savior when I was twelve years old. By that time, I was playing the piano for Sunday school classes at the First Presbyterian Church in Lake City, Florida. I attended my minister's confirmation class, where we were taught the message of salvation through Jesus Christ. He told us what it meant to follow Him and to give our lives to Him. We then appeared before the church body and publicly declared our decision to accept Him as Lord and Savior. I did this, but I had known Jesus from those earliest days when my mother told me about Him. I even remember being in Sunday school as a three-year-old and knowing that Jesus loved me.

A few years later, "You want me to walk down with you?" my friend asked. She had invited me to a revival meeting at her Baptist church. The sermon touched my heart, and I was in tears. We walked to the altar together and I reaffirmed my decision for Christ.

Throughout my growing-up years, the Lord made it possible for my parents to pay for my piano lessons. It wasn't easy during the Depression. God was so good to provide for my music education, making it possible for me to become the church musician I am today.

Even though I took a lot of wrong turns in the course of my life, the Lord was always watching over me and drew me back to Himself.

The work of the Holy Spirit has permeated every aspect of my music ministry. Many times someone will tell me how a particular piece of music blessed them in a special way. One time a woman came up to me after a communion service and said, "Today was the birthday of my deceased husband. He loved to play special hymns on the piano. During the communion, you played all of his favorite hymns: 'Amazing Grace,' 'Blessed Assurance,' and all the others he loved." Only God could plan that through the power of the Holy Spirit.

There is a beautiful contemporary song about the heart of worship. The song's focus is whether or not I have made my life to be about Jesus instead of myself.

All of this helps me remember why we church organists are here and why we choose the music we do. It's all about God and our worship of Him. We are truly fulfilling a calling of the Lord. Scripture tells us "Do your best to present yourself to God as one approved." That doesn't mean just the part of our lives that we would catalog as "spiritual" but also involves our duties in our vocations and avocations. We are accountable to Him in every part of our lives, and more so when we are a part of a ministry to His people.

As church musicians it is important to keep that perspective. When we focus on the worship of God as our primary purpose, we not only have the inspiration from Him that we need to fulfill that calling, but we also are better able to keep every part of our lives in order.

CHAPTER 3

Practice Plus

Training Time

I HAD PLAYED PIANO FOR SUNDAY school since I was twelve years old. Finally, at age sixteen, I had an opportunity to play an organ. Our church invested in a Hammond electronic instrument. The Hammond had sounds that attempted to mimic the pipe organ, giving smaller churches such as ours the opportunity to afford an organ without great expense.

I was enthralled just by looking at this marvelous instrument with its two keyboards and all those pedals. And not only that, but our church had the distinction of having an excellent church organist. On Wednesday afternoons he was featured live on our local radio station, playing popular music for fifteen minutes on our church's Hammond. That was so exciting to me.

It wasn't long before I had a terrific crush on our organist, whose musical skills mesmerized me. I hung around whenever he was practicing and watched him make that organ "talk."

When I was a sophomore in high school, a special opportunity came my way. The church organist said to me, "My family and I are taking a two-week vacation this summer. I would like you to play the organ for those two Sundays."

I was fearful, not knowing what to do. He gave me what must have been the world's shortest lesson in organ-playing on a Hammond: "Just press the G on the left for the sound you need to play the hymns, press the F to accompany the choir's anthem, and don't worry about the pedals." I did it, and everything went fine. From that moment on I was hooked and had permission to play our church's Hammond from time to time.

When I enrolled at the University of Florida as a freshman, I concentrated on my books for the first year. When I entered my sophomore year, though, I signed up for organ lessons with the university organist, Claude Murphree. He taught his organ students much in technique as well as about how to handle different organs. We studied on the huge pipe organ in the university auditorium, the smaller pipe organ in the student union building, and the Hammond in the music building with its paper-thin walls. Sometimes when I was practicing the organ in the closet-sized room, a trumpet player would be practicing his scales next door. What a competition that was. In order to hear our own music, we each had to play at full volume.

For the remainder of my time at the university, I studied with Claude. When I was a junior, he found me a job with a tiny Lutheran congregation who met in a converted home. That was my first experience as a working organist. I certainly was not good at keeping the schedule. Many times when I slept late on a Sunday morning, I would run madly across campus and arrive breathlessly at the church while the pastor was standing on the lawn looking at his watch. That congregation suffered a lot from my inexperience, but they were always kind.

At that time, the University of Florida offered no music degrees. I was attending school on a scholarship given to produce teachers, so I had to enroll in the College of Education. I graduated with a BAE in secondary education, majoring in English with a minor in mathematics. Having been in a band since seventh grade, I also played flute and piccolo in the Gator Band, along with many others who were pursuing degrees in other colleges.

I would love to have received a music degree, but that was not to be. I have improved my craft through the years by studying on my own. Once, I took a course in music theory to fulfill my teacher recertification requirement. I have attended many music conferences, taking advantage of the opportunities to gain more knowledge.

My education in organ at the university has brought me life-long joy as well as income for my family and me. After graduation, I taught one year of seventh-grade music and math. Later I did some substitute teaching in high schools while I was a stay-at-home mom. But for many years, the organ has been a constant in my life.

I began my career as a church organist with a volunteer situation. Three years after my husband and I graduated from college, we attended Eastminster Presbyterian Church in Indialantic, Florida, a small community on the coast east of Melbourne. Their organist had purchased a Baldwin electronic for the church. When she discovered that I was a trained organist, she decided to retire from her position and, with the blessing of the minister, asked me to take on the job.

There was no budget for an organist's salary, so my predecessor decided to give me her personal check for ten dollars every week. That was a boon for my small family and me. The church later included an organist's stipend in their budget. At that point, I became a salaried professional organist, although at the same rate of pay.

When I began there, it was difficult to find time to practice. I was teaching school and had a two-year-old child. The pastor said, "The congregation loves to hear their favorite special numbers again. Don't worry about needing to set up new pieces all the time." He was a sweet man and a calming influence.

I remained at that position for the next thirteen years, until we moved to Orlando. During that time, I also served as organist for Brevard Light Opera and the many musicals they produced for the community. I supplemented our income by teaching organ at the church and piano lessons at home. I also played for many weddings and funerals at our church and other churches.

Brevard Engineering College (now Florida Institute of Technology) was located in Melbourne, and the president asked me to play for their graduation ceremonies each year. A special blessing came my way when I played for the processional as the late astronaut, Major Virgil "Gus" I. Grissom, received a well-deserved Doctor of Space Science degree. One of my proudest possessions is the program for that ceremony with Gus Grissom's autograph and my name as organist. It was quite an honor to meet him and shake his hand.

After arriving in Orlando, I sat out for a year. Then our elder son's music teacher had to recommend someone for an organist position at an area church. At that time, she had no student who had reached that level, so she called me. I had missed the joy of creating music and immediately accepted the job. It was great to get back to my love of music as my focus. After that, I continued my church organ career for many years. Now that I'm retired, I substitute regularly for my fellow organist friends at several different local churches and enjoy it very much.

Personal Benefits

Many people spend their time trying to find the next high or discover their ultimate delight in life. I believe an organist has no problem finding it. "Strapping on the organ" and living in the moment brings me the ultimate in happiness. It's not unusual for me to begin practicing a beautiful classic written by Bach or Pachelbel and discover that half a day has gone by. Sometimes I get up from practice to drink some water and walk a little, only to find that I've been playing the organ for four hours without a break.

I've learned to devote some practice time to working ahead of my more immediate schedule. In addition, I like to work on a special piece that I find challenging, whether or not I plan to use it in a service.

Practice time should include the ABCs of organ work—such as the standard "hands together/pedal alone/left hand with pedal/right hand with pedal" routines. All that nitty-gritty work is useful. Then it's time to launch into the interpretation of the piece and prepare to get out its message. That, of course, also involves choosing the stops (sounds) needed for each part and practicing the changing of the stops.

Playing the organ has brought me many personal benefits. I gain great fulfillment from conquering a special piece of music that requires many hours of practice and have a true sense of satisfaction in accomplishing that task. Learning music that glorifies God and presenting it to the best of one's ability is the true mission for the Christian artist.

I also find playing the organ relaxing and therapeutic. When I feel melancholy or distressed, spending hours at the organ playing beautiful music brings healing.

One of the most difficult times of my life occurred when my husband and I were in the process of a divorce. I went to the church and spent hours immersed in the glorious sounds of the organ. It eased my soul and spirit. As the beauty of the Franck *Third Organ Chorale* filled the sanctuary, my heart soared to the throne room of God. I felt His peace drifting into my soul and spirit.

I experienced other days so joyful I could only express the feeling at the organ. Of course, one of those times was when the Lord brought my husband and me back together again. I would enjoy playing hymns such as "Great is Thy Faithfulness." When our children and grandchildren were born, my choices of music for the church services also expressed the joy of life. I chose for the postludes numbers such as Pachelbel's "Toccata in E Minor" or Marcello's "Psalm XIX."

It is easy for me to agree with doctors who have realized that music indeed "soothes the savage breast."

CHAPTER 4

Faux Pas

THERE WERE TIMES WHEN I wished I had a particular service back again. "Another chance, Lord, if you please." Unfortunately, that isn't possible, and so we go on.

When I was young and inexperienced, it only took one or two services in which I had problems to remind me to pay more attention to the number of verses of a hymn. I felt embarrassed to look out at the confused faces of the congregation when I launched into one more verse. The problem was they had just sung the final verse. Gulp. All I could do at that point was bravely play it through.

That is the reason I learned to sing along on the hymns. That way, I always know where we are. The additional plus is that I reflect the phrasing of the words correctly. Sometimes someone will say, "I love to see you singing as you play the hymns." I smile. They need never know my original reason for doing that. I also discovered that I enjoy singing along.

Early in my career, some events occurred that underscored to me my need for diligent practice on each special solo number. One time as we finished a church service, the sweet, loving pastor said to the congregation, "Joanna always plays such a beautiful postlude. I want you to remain seated and listen to it today."

Horrors. That morning, I had grabbed a piece I hardly knew. Not having spent enough time on it, I bumbled through. I'm sure the congregation wondered if the pastor had lost his mind. I could see the reaction on some of their faces. A couple of them looked embarrassed and others, bored. I could imagine their thoughts: "And we'll be late to lunch for this? Forget it." That thought caused me to miss more notes and magnify the problem.

The other music that day reflected my hours of practice. But I left church that morning humbled and resolved to come prepared for every part of any future services in which I was involved. I never again thought of the postlude as a throwaway piece.

II. THE FAMILY OF GOD:
ORGAN MINISTRY IN THE CHURCH

CHAPTER 5

Organ Committees

ORGAN COMMITTEES ARE FASCINATING entities that exist for the purpose of researching and choosing an organ for a church. They take on a life of their own—usually the life of the chairman. In two churches where I've worked, I had the experience of working with that dedicated group. In each of those cases, the church was dealing with an old, tired, electronic instrument. One church was in the market for an electronic model, and the other preferred a pipe organ.

In the first instance, the chairman was a sharp businessman with no musical background. One person in the group, a choir member, was the only musician who served on the committee. He told me the other members asked him what they should do about the ancient electronic organ.

He replied, "Take an ax and chop it up."

He had an accurate assessment of its value.

The committee then made arrangements for me to join them to play three organs they were considering. What fun that was—especially because one member of the group flew us from Melbourne to Orlando in his private plane. After we had visited those installments, I told the committee members, "The three-manual Allen would be a wonderful choice. It has the versatility we need as well as beautiful sounds."

The chairman called me one day. "We plan to make a decision this week."

"Shouldn't you wait until the minister comes back from his trip?"

"No," he said. "We don't have to wait for that. I suppose you want him back because he supports *your* choice."

That was blunt. Incidentally, he was correct.

The committee did choose the Allen. Before the final decision, the chairman and I had another conversation. "This is a wonderful instrument," I said. "It has the best sound."

"We're not buying sound. We're buying warranty."

That statement startled me.

He said he asked the committee to choose the Allen because the store owner was "a good businessman," and he admired that. I thanked the Lord that it was also the instrument with the best sound.

I had an interesting experience with another church that was considering a pipe organ. They had abandoned the idea ten years earlier. At that time, they failed to get the support of the entire congregation.

But from the time the church sanctuary was built, some people had dreamed of a pipe organ. The building had been designed with space for the pipes to be installed at a later date. Organ chambers waited on each side of the pulpit area. The low hum of that hope had played in their thoughts and hearts for years. And now, a few forward-thinking individuals knew this was the time.

During the church's period of deliberation, the committee was considering the possibility of a clock on the organ console. I discussed that with one of the members.

"A digital clock would be a good choice," I said.

He responded, "Oh, no. It has to be analog. I don't like digital. With digital the organist can't tell how many minutes it is before the service begins." That was a strange comment, especially because he was speaking to the organist—the one who would be using it. Intriguing. And by the way, there was no clock on the pipe organ the church later installed.

What a great day when the pipes arrived! The congregation was invited to take part in the long-awaited event. Under the supervision of the Reuter specialists, they lined up to pick up pipes, large and small, and take them into the sanctuary. My teenage grandson, Samuel, was a part of the big day. Everyone had a wonderful time.

I was fortunate to be on staff when all the plans came together. Before I moved on to another church, I had the exquisite joy of playing that Reuter pipe organ for an entire year.

CHAPTER 6

The Honeymoon Period

SINCE MY COLLEGE DAYS MORE than fifty years ago, I have had five different church organist jobs, with a year-long break after our family moved to Orlando and a later break of several months. In each church, I experienced a honeymoon period when I was new. I had an opportunity at that time to speak up when I needed something to help me do my job better. I found that the church leaders were willing to make any changes that would assist me.

At one church, I interviewed with the choir director in the sanctuary. I noticed the organ's position behind a waist-high wooden panel that obscured it. Because the organ was set below floor level with the organist facing the choir and the back wall, I had no way to see the congregation or the main church aisle when seated on the bench.

I asked the choir director, "How did your organist see a bride when she was coming in the door?"

He answered, "Oh, someone would tell her, probably the soloist."

I said, "I'll need a mirror. Sometimes there's no soloist, and I can't fly blind. I'll need to see what's happening in the church."

I suggested two large circular or rectangular mirrors in the two corners behind the choir. The deacons didn't care for that idea, so they worked together to try to figure out how to provide a mirror without making it too obvious.

They came up with an ingenious plan, installing a long mirror about five inches tall along the top of the wall behind the choir and next to the ceiling. The mirror was tilted at an angle so I could see the back of the church from the organ bench. As the crowning glory, the mirror was decorated with gold curlicues throughout its length. This satisfied the deacons' desire for semi-obscurity and beauty and filled my need to see behind me.

At another church, I discovered the same problem right away. From my position at the organ, I couldn't see the back of the church. The organ sat at one side of the chancel, but half of it rested below the level of the raised chancel floor.

During my interview with the music committee I asked, "How did your previous organist see a bride coming in the door?"

The committee members chuckled, and one person said, "Well, he was rather short, and he stood on the pedals to look for her."

"I'll need to have the organ higher so I can see the back of the church."

They came up with a plan. They built a platform the level of the chancel floor and moved the organ onto it. The next Sunday as I began to play, I heard a thumping noise whenever I hit a pedal note. It was annoying, but I didn't know if the congregation could hear it, so I continued to thump away. The empty, box-like structure under the organ made a great drum—not the desired sound when playing the pedals.

Again, someone came up with a solution. They blew some fiberglass insulation into the empty space and—voilà—mission accomplished. I appreciated having church leaders who not only cared but were great problem-solvers, too.

CHAPTER 7
The Nuts and Bolts of the Job

HAVING NO AVAILABLE TIMEPIECE could handicap me at the organ. If there was no clock on the console, no watch on my wrist, and no clock in the church, I did a lot of guesswork. I could always check the time with the pastor or the choir director before my prelude and take it from there. I could never find a suitable, inexpensive (emphasis on inexpensive) clock to bring with me to a wedding or any other service.

One day, my watch wristband broke. I began to bring the watch in my purse and lay it on the console. Later, someone gave an anonymous donation through the church so I could purchase a wristband. It was a relief to be accurate again. However, a small quiet clock with a large face would have worked just as well.

Of course, choir robes made up another important element of my organist duties. When I had a weekly job at the same church, I had to wear a choir robe. My robe was made differently from those the choir members wore. An organist's robe usually has sleeves that fasten with a snap or Velcro at the wrists to keep them from interfering with arm movement or hanging loose and catching on the edges of the keys. Its shorter length prevents the robe from slipping under the organist's feet and causing errors when playing the pedals.

Now that I'm retired and substitute often at different churches, I feel freer to ask if I can play in street clothes without a robe. Usually, the choir director will agree, and I then wear a pantsuit that coordinates with the colors in the church or the colors of the season of the church calendar. That frees me to play without concern for the flowing robe problem. For weddings, I wear a pantsuit in the color(s) the bride has chosen for her big occasion.

Another important detail is the purchase of organ shoes. Early in my career, I attended a music seminar. The instructor told us, "It is very important to have the correct shoes for playing the organ. I recommend the Capezio tap shoe. I suggest that you buy a pair and remove the taps."

I couldn't work those shoes into my budget for quite a while. But at last I could get the correct pair for my organ playing, a kind specifically made for organists. Such a delight! These shoes have special soles that grip the pedals and yet slide easily from one pedal to another. They also have a high enough heel so that there is a gap between the heel and the pad of the foot. That allows the organist to play a note with the heel and then skip over a pedal to play another note with the toe, or vice versa.

The shoe for female organists is the Mary Jane-style shoe, which buckles on. The big plus factor is that I can order it in different colors. I began in the early days with black shoes, but now I enjoy being a twinkle-toes, and I wear silver ones just for fun. Of course, there are concert artists who love unique shoes with rhinestones and special colors. Feeling flashy? Wear those. Demure and proper? Stick with black.

CHAPTER 8

Balancing Act

JUGGLING WORK DAYS WITH organist duties and the everyday tasks of a wife and mother of four can be difficult, but it can be done. I consider myself living proof.

Whenever a funeral was scheduled, usually on a workday, I asked off work, either as part of vacation time or by staying over in the evenings to make up the missed hours. Sometimes the funeral was held a few miles from town, so that meant more time off.

Once, a woman who was a longtime member of our church died. Her family asked me to come to a funeral home and cemetery that were about ten miles away. I had to smile, because this was a lady who had no love for the church's music department. In fact, I received a report on my first Sunday at that church that she had covered her ears when my prelude went above the volume of pianissimo, the softest of sounds.

I asked off work to have time for the funeral and arrived early to practice with one of the granddaughters, who would sing a solo during the service. I said a silent hooray when the lady's daughter asked for my address. I hadn't discussed a fee with the family, so I was glad to hear that she planned to send me something. In my mind, that translated to the word *check*. I was delighted to receive compensation for my time off from work.

Within a couple of weeks, the daughter sent a nice thank-you note—without a check. After that incident, I learned to speak up to either the pastor of the church or to the family member and quote a fee in advance. We were feeding four active teenagers and needed the income, but that policy also made it easier for everyone. If they found the amount unacceptable, I would say, "I can help you find an organist." That way I didn't get caught doing a job that took me away from my family, my work, or other activities without compensation for my time. I always followed through by giving them names and phone numbers of other organists who might be available.

Years later, I served as organist for a church that had taken care of the money issue by establishing wedding and funeral fees for the organist, sexton, minister, and use of the church. The church administrator met with the family and gave them a paper that explained the costs involved. Later, the administrator collected the total and dispersed the funds. That simple blessing saved me a lot of grief.

I always considered Wednesday or Thursday night rehearsals a treat, even though I worked a forty- or fifty-hour week at my day job. Those nights meant socializing with those wonderful people who serve as volunteer choir members. I loved their company and found them to be dedicated, talented, friendly, and loving. I always enjoyed walking into a choir practice and greeting them. We have shared our joys and sorrows and prayed with and for each other often. Many of them have also been family friends through the years.

CHAPTER 9

Traditional or Contemporary

IN SOME CHURCHES, THE people in the congregation enter into major discussions concerning whether the church should sing and play traditional or contemporary music. When that's a big problem, the choral director and the organist can defuse it a bit by planning music that touches both areas.

As the organist in that situation, I would sometimes play a contemporary arrangement of a favorite hymn. Then I could end the service with a rouser of a postlude by a composer such as Bach or Marcello. The music director would plan to use an old chestnut choir number one Sunday and an upbeat contemporary special the next.

Many churches provide a choice for the congregation, as in one church I served. The early-morning service was contemporary music with the youth choir leading the service. The later service (at the old-time conventional hour for church, 11:00 a.m.) was in the classical and hymnal mode with a traditional choir.

I appreciate both types of services. I enjoy playing many of the contemporary pieces and was pleased to use my piano skills often in the early service. But the traditional service gave me the opportunity to play many beautiful organ pieces written by the old masters. I had the blessing to receive my education from a university organist who was brilliant in both areas and gave his students experience in both. He taught us to respect all types of organ music.

CHAPTER 10
Dante Who

MY ESTEEMED ORGAN PROFESSOR, Claude Murphree, taught all his students the importance of having the titles of our music and composers' names printed in the church's bulletins. I tried to be diligent about giving that information to the church secretary each week. If I hadn't dropped a note by the office in time, I would sometimes make a phone call.

One week I called Jean, the church secretary, close to her deadline for the information. I hadn't given her the title of the offertory.

"Jean, my offertory will be 'Andante' by Wilson."

"Thanks. I'm just putting the bulletin together."

It was quite a surprise on Sunday to discover that the offertory would probably be a rousing piece of music dedicated to a special general who led an unknown battle. Somehow it was printed in the bulletin as "On Dante."

I never phoned in my information again, even if I had to get in the car and drive a few miles to hand the church secretary a typewritten or carefully printed note spelling out the titles and composers' names. Thank the good Lord that with the advent of email, that job has now become simpler.

CHAPTER 11

Church Life and Relationships

THERE SHOULD BE NO disconnect between the organist and the congregation; in fact, I believe the organist should be a part of regular church activities. Even as a non-member, I found it wise to attend church functions such as potluck dinners, student recitals and shows, or other events.

By joining in, I became more knowledgeable about the choir members with whom I often worked. It was a real plus to attend a congregational talent show and discover that the primary tenor was a stand-up comic or that one of the quiet teens in the youth choir played a mean saxophone.

All that interaction created a real camaraderie between the congregation and me. Not only was it enjoyable, but—let's face it—it had a positive effect on job security. Yes, I developed "fans" among the congregation because I was a part of them. But the feeling was mutual, because I developed many friendships in the congregations where I served.

Once a pastor told me, "Thank you for staying in the sanctuary during the service. The last organist would leave during my sermon and only return when it was time for the last hymn."

What a slap in the face that is to a minister. I believe an organist should support the priest or pastor in every possible way. I always felt that pastors have to encounter enough criticism, and the organist has no need to add to that.

One time a pastor told me, "I feel so impressed that you are being attentive and writing notes during my sermon." I was paying attention, but I didn't have the heart to tell him the full story. Yes, I was taking copious notes on his sermon in shorthand. But I did so primarily because I was enrolled in a shorthand class and needed the experience. Should I have confessed? I think not.

My husband agreed with me about church participation. Even when he and the children attended the church where we were members, he accompanied me to many functions at whichever church I served as organist. At one of those, he became a regular at a men's Bible study and prayer group. He continued with them for years, even when I had gone on to serve as the organist at another church.

CHAPTER 12
Surely the Presence

THERE IS SO MUCH MORE to playing the organ than reading the notes on the page. After all the practice to get every measure right comes the interpretation, the message of the music.

Some have told me they appreciate the way I play hymns—not only referring to those played for congregational singing but also the quiet music accompanying a communion service.

Particularly poignant was an occasion when I was practicing for a funeral. The service was scheduled to begin within two hours. I was playing a lovely praise song called "Surely the Presence of the Lord Is in This Place." As I played, I felt the words of the song and experienced His presence, a true time of personal worship. While I played, the family had entered the narthex to place pictures and other mementos there. When I finished that piece, I stopped to set up another number.

"Please play that again" came the voice of a man nearby.

Unbeknown to me, the elderly widower had come into the sanctuary and was walking back and forth across the front, weeping as he passed the casket that held the body of his beautiful wife. He felt the powerful message of the music just as I had.

I played the piece once more. When I finished, he asked for it again.

My heart went out to him as he grieved. I continued to play until his daughter came forward and asked him to come get ready. He was reluctant to leave but went with her. How happy it made me to soothe his hurting heart through my music. That's what completes us as organists and shows us the reasons we're musicians, bringing to our consciousness the way our music serves God Himself. We're using the talents He gave us so we can give them back to Him—and help the hurting soul.

Later that same year, I played that beautiful music again for the widower at his own funeral service.

III. COUNT YOUR BLESSINGS:

PERSONAL AND PROFESSIONAL SUPPORT

CHAPTER 13

Family Ties

Hugh's Support

LIFE IS SIMPLER FOR A part-time organist who has the encouragement of family. My husband supports my organ playing. He appreciates the fact that I'm doing work I enjoy, and it doesn't hurt that my playing brings in extra money for the family.

For many years, I had a full-time forty-hour job as a secretary in addition to working as a church organist. I often had to spend my evenings at the church practicing. Hugh always came with me and brought along some paperwork. After a while, he would stretch out on a choir pew and go to sleep while I worked away. He has spent many hours napping on church pews.

I spent most of one Saturday at a church practicing with a children's choir and their director. Hugh came along with me and sat on a back pew with his papers. After we practiced songs with one group of children, another group came in the back door and walked up the aisle to practice in the front. One of the children pulled at the director's sleeve and whispered to her, "There's a man sleeping on the back pew."

She answered, "It's OK. It's just the organist's husband."

During the years that I was working seven days a week—full-time as a secretary and part-time as an organist—my husband took over the housekeeping. Sometimes I would skip a Saturday practice-time if I had prepared music in advance. Then we could take a day trip or do something else as a family.

Hugh did all the grocery shopping and loved it so much that he continues to this day. He considers it his responsibility to buy healthy foods inexpensively, and he does it well. The training he received while growing up was a distinct advantage to us all our married lives. His grandfather founded an IGA grocery store in Sebring, Florida. When Hugh was old enough, he worked at the IGA under the supervision of his two uncles, and he grew up learning how to select fresh vegetables and good meat. His father was the butcher, and for a while his family lived in the old homestead just behind the grocery store. So our family has always been in good hands with Hugh doing the shopping.

After Hugh retired he made all the family's suppers and usually prepared a lunch for me to take to work. He liked to say, "I make a lunch, hand it to Joanna, push her out the door and say, 'Go. Make money.'"

When I finally retired from my job with Orange County, I wondered if I would ever get my kitchen back. It wasn't "my" kitchen anymore—it was Hugh's. It took a while, but he finally decided that he likes sitting in the living room, reading the newspaper, and watching television while I prepare dinner. When I first began cooking, he would hover around and say, "What I do with that is . . ." I'm glad he has settled down now and enjoys having me wait on him.

Support from the Children

There never has been any question about our four children's support of my organist jobs. They grew up with me playing the organ, and it was the only lifestyle they knew. The routine for the children went like this: We go to church on Sundays. We are in the nursery or in Sunday school, and then we are either in church for the service or in the nursery while Mother plays the organ.

I usually resumed my organ job after the latest baby was about six weeks old. My routine after the birth of my fourth child involved juggling a diaper bag and baby plus a two- and a four-year old while getting them and a seven-year-old dressed and into the car with my husband and me—all in time for Sunday school. Then I practiced with the choir and played for the church service.

Sometimes I took the children with me when practicing the organ on a Saturday. At Eastminster Presbyterian Church, the organ and choir were situated in a gallery at the back of the church. The gallery was twenty feet above floor level, and on each side was a long spiral staircase for access to the choir loft. When the three youngest children were between five and nine years old, I handed them coloring and story books so they could sit downstairs and occupy their time while I practiced. Sometimes they would come up and down the spiral staircases just for fun. My daughter Shirley was in her forties before she told me, "By the way, Mom, you remember that spiral staircase? One time I climbed on the outside of the staircase, holding tightly to the railing over that twenty-foot drop." Meanwhile, I was blissfully creating music and unaware of her peril. It still makes me cringe to think of it.

Our children could all understand the delight and the chore of practicing music. David studied piano and trumpet, Tom was a percussionist, Shirley played flute, and Diane played clarinet and was in her high school handbell choir. All of them sang in the church choirs. We all supported one another's skills and went to every concert and football game to cheer each other on.

Sometimes, people asked what instrument Hugh played. We always answered, "The radio and the phonograph." However, he loves to demonstrate that he can find middle C on the piano.

Hugh was the capable manager of the whole family, making sure we could all coordinate our schedules, grab the correct uniforms and other clothing, and get to the various functions on time. There were times when we raced out the door and started driving away, only to turn around and go back for the instrument. Before long, we learned to ask, "Do you have your flute (drumsticks, trumpet, clarinet)?" It's amazing how you can forget the major instrument in your rush to put everything else together. At least in my career, I never had to worry about leaving the organ behind. I just went to the church and there it was.

All four children have been wonderful supporters. When we moved to Orlando, I played at three different churches in succession as they grew up. We belonged to a Presbyterian church. The children worshiped there with their dad while I played the organ across town at a United Methodist church. Later, I became organist at Reeves United Methodist church, only about ten blocks from our home, and after that at Winter Park Presbyterian Church. I was associate organist at the Cathedral Church of St. Luke before retiring.

Whenever the choir I accompanied presented a special evening program, my family would attend, which always boosted my morale. I missed being in Sunday-morning church with them but had wonderful family experiences with the choir members. However, one of my happiest memories occurred one Mother's Day. I slipped onto the organ bench to begin the prelude, looked up, and saw two of my college-age children. Tom and Diane gave me the biggest smiles, and their presence was a blessing I'll never forget.

CHAPTER 14

Our Professional Organization

Serving in the Chapter

THE DAY FINALLY CAME when I joined my professional organization—the American Guild of Organists (AGO). I had been a student member in college but did not join as a full member for several more years. After college, my life was filled with marriage, starting a family, and dealing with a tight budget. I didn't realize how much I was missing by not making the effort to get involved in AGO.

The benefits of joining AGO are tremendous. I have enjoyed meeting and becoming friends with my colleagues as we share our expertise in various fields. Our membership includes not only professional recitalists and those with degrees in organ but also part-time organists, music directors, amateurs, and others who love organs and organ music. We plan programs, concerts, and recitals to help the members gain more knowledge about our craft and present these for the public to educate them about the beauty of organ music.

"When shall we do Pedals, Pipes, and Pizza?" someone on the Executive Committee asked during one planning meeting to select programs for the upcoming year. The next question was, "Where will it be?"

We discussed possibilities of date and place. "Let's ask about St. Andrew's in Sanford. They have a pipe organ and a school. We can invite all the children from the school as well as students of local piano teachers to come for that Saturday half-day."

After receiving permission for the location and settling on a date, we hosted children who learned about pipe organs, had an opportunity to play one, and then enjoyed pizza. They paid nothing for the experience. What a great day! By presenting PPP (Pedals, Pipes, and Pizza) each year, we encourage children to love the instrument. Perhaps some will become organists one day.

Any member gets much more out of membership in AGO as an active participant—serving on a committee, helping with projects, and volunteering to run for office. I've benefited in many ways by being part of the Executive Committee in my local AGO chapter, helping plan events and giving input about how we organize and run the chapter activities. One of my special jobs is mailing out chapter information to those few members who don't have email (our snail-mailers). The fellowship and camaraderie with my fellow members enriches my life.

Conferences

One of the exciting events our local chapter sponsored was the Southeast Region AGO conference in 1993. It was a privilege to meet with other organists and choir directors from the southeastern states. We arranged for workshops, concerts, transportation, and many activities. The participants expressed their gratitude for all our hard work in preparing for the conference.

Afterward, we received many compliments: "What a great conference! Thank you especially for the wonderful transportation that you arranged to take us from our hotel to every event." "We enjoyed all the concerts you planned—they were beautiful and inspiring." "What outstanding organists! This was my first opportunity to hear a couple of these world-class performers." "It was such a pleasure to hear the different pipe organs in your city."

Some of our members attend the National AGO Conference, held in different parts of the country every two years. The various regional conferences are held every two years in between the national conferences. The national conference works with a much larger budget and has the opportunity to invite major recitalists from all over the world. It also presents many workshops with leaders from different parts of the country.

In Touch

By staying in contact with other AGO members in my area, I receive information whenever they are playing in a recital or presenting a special program at their church or in the community. Our chapter has a website (www.CFAGO.org) that keeps us informed about our own activities and other programs of interest in the community and around the state. We also publish a monthly dean's letter that we email to the local members. The dean of the chapter is the officer whose position is equivalent to the office of president in other organizations.

Our chapter's yearbook is vital. When we renew our membership every year, we have the opportunity to list in the yearbook our availability for various functions: weddings, worship services, and funerals. Current teachers can be listed in the Organ Teachers list. The yearbook also contains all the members' names and contact information.

Our National Magazine and Website

Our AGO national organization publishes a monthly magazine, *The American Organist (TAO),* that we also consider important. It informs us of opportunities to advance in our professional lives through various degrees of accomplishment by passing the requirements for a professional certification.

Our magazine also contains articles of interest that will enhance our careers or may feature a special pipe organ installation with beautiful pictures, a list of the stops on that organ, the story of the inspiration to have it built, and information about the current organist and the builder. The cover picture of that special organ is always beautiful. We can also enjoy write-ups of the lives of composers and targeted ads telling us of the upcoming performances of world-renowned organists. Included is a classified section advertising available organist or choir director jobs. Our local AGO chapter sends pictures and information to be published about our activities.

It's not unusual to walk into an AGO meeting and hear "Did you read the newest *TAO*? There's an article about the City of Cleveland, Ohio celebrating the organ with events and concerts all over the city." or "Don't forget to check the *TAO* for the report from the national convention—and by the way, the write-up of our members' concert is in the Chapter News section."

In addition to our chapter dean's letter, chapter website, and the *TAO,* we also have access to the national AGO website (www.agohq.org) where we find information of overall interest to members everywhere.

Our Special Motto

A big plus with the AGO is that from its beginning, the founders realized that their love for music and their skills came from the source of all things good—God Himself. AGO's motto is the Latin phrase *Soli Deo Gloria*—"to God be the glory." This is the statement that Johann Sebastian Bach wrote at the conclusion of each masterpiece he produced. AGO members have the desire to glorify God as we present our music, whether in a church setting or a recital hall.

Moving Right Along

I have not only gained much knowledge about our profession through the AGO, but I've formed lasting friendships with other members through participation in various events and programs. Another plus: now that I've retired, I receive calls from my friends in AGO whenever they need me to substitute at the organ for them. "Joanna, I need you for the second Sunday next month. Are you available?" "Help! Our organist was called out of town on a family emergency. Could you come next Sunday?" It's a pleasure to visit their different churches and work with their friendly and well-trained choirs. I get the opportunity to play different organs in the community. It's a wonderful way to enjoy retirement.

IV. THE BOND OF LOVE:
PLAYING FOR WEDDINGS

CHAPTER 15

Eazy Money

I BET THAT'S THE EASIEST money *you* ever earned." I could not miss the look of disdain on the man's face as he handed me ten dollars. I stood there in shock, mumbled a quick "Thank you," and headed out the door.

As a church organist in the mid-1960s, I earned very little for weddings and funerals— usually only fifteen dollars for a wedding when a rehearsal night was involved and ten dollars when playing for the wedding alone.

At the time of the incident, I was in my mid-thirties, a divorcée with four children. This took place before the Lord brought my husband and me together again and renewed our marriage.

That day, I had received a desperate phone call.

"Mrs. Wallace, could you come to our church to play for a wedding? The wedding party is here, and we don't have an organist."

The church was on the mainland in Melbourne. When I heard that a bride was waiting and there was no organist, I rushed to call my babysitter. I drove across the causeway from the beach side, praying the bridge that separated my home from the city would not be up. Never having played at that church before, I hurried to get there in order to be as early as possible. Arriving just in time to look over the organ console, I quickly decided what stops to use. Beginning with prelude music, I then played the wedding marches for the ceremony itself.

The man who handed me the money was a member of the family who had waited in the narthex after the wedding. He must have estimated the time I was at the church and decided I was overpaid.

If I had time to think, perhaps I could have come up with a snappy answer: "No, sir. Not easy. It took me more than twenty-five years of training and experience to have the ability to jump into a car and dash over here to play the wedding without advance notice. Part of the ten dollars will be paid to my babysitter. I've also given up time with my children to help you out." Wouldn't it be nice to have a great comeback whenever we needed one? Giving a response like that would have been much better than kicking him in the shins. I did neither.

As with most experiences, the Lord used that day's adventure to help someone else. Later, I accompanied for a soloist. We were walking up to the church where she had been asked to sing, having gone over her solos a few times the day before.

She said, "I really don't feel prepared for this."

"Yes, you do. You've prepared for this morning for the last twenty-five years. It will be beautiful."

Her face and posture relaxed, and she blessed the group that morning with the glorious richness of her voice.

Many times the Lord has brought a special scripture to my mind. This passage has blessed me, and I love sharing it with others. "Praise be to the God and Father of our Lord Jesus Christ, the Father of compassion and the God of all comfort, who comforts us in all our troubles, so that we can comfort those in any trouble with the comfort we ourselves receive from God" (2 Corinthians 1:3-4).

CHAPTER 16

Counting the Cost

I PLAYED FOR ONE WEDDING at my home church during the summer after my junior year of college. I used the Hammond, the first organ I had ever played. I felt at ease because not only did I know the wedding party and the entire congregation, but I had enough organ pieces in my repertoire to cover a wedding. I did not know anything about charging a fee—I was just thrilled to be able to do it. Since I was planning to be married that year as well, the bride presented me with a gift of four crystal iced tea glasses in my chosen pattern.

During the spring semester at the University of Florida earlier that year, I received a request to play for a wedding in Gainesville. One Sunday when I was finishing the postlude at the small Lutheran church where I played, a young lady (who did not usually attend the church) said to me, "The pastor said I could use the church organist for my wedding." So we discussed when and where her wedding would be. I did not give a second thought to the way she worded her statement until much later.

The wedding was scheduled to take place at a United Methodist Church just off campus. I consulted with Claude Murphree, and he helped me work up thirty minutes of music from the pieces I had already learned. We also prepared the marches for the processions. He gave me a bit of advice: "As you play, turn each book upside down beside you on the organ bench so that if you need more music, you can pick up the books and begin the set again at the beginning." That turned out to be invaluable information.

I went to that church and became familiar with the organ. The soloist, Candy, and I practiced her songs. The rehearsal went well, and we also attended the rehearsal dinner. We were both good musicians but naïve about discussing fees. We talked about it and wondered if the family planned to give us gifts for our services or whether we might receive checks instead.

At the rehearsal dinner, the bride and groom handed out gifts to all their attendants. We felt rather conspicuous because we didn't know anybody. We were even strangers to one another until we practiced together. Since we did not receive a gift at the rehearsal dinner, we assumed we would each receive a check for our part.

The next day Candy and I were at the organ early. I set up my music and began to play the prelude music thirty minutes before the ceremony was to begin. As I was finishing the last number I asked Candy, "Do you see her out there yet?" She didn't, but she kept looking.

The bride was nowhere in sight when I finished the thirty-minute prelude, so, breathing a prayer of thanks for my professor's wonderful advice, I turned over the entire set of music and began again. I kept checking with Candy. She continued to look for the bride and finally whispered that she was in view just as I was finishing the last piece. I had played a one-hour prelude recital. I began the marches, and everything went smoothly.

That was toward the end of my school year. During that summer, I waited to hear from the bride's mother, expecting a check for playing for her daughter's wedding. Nothing. I also waited for a thank-you note from the bride because I had bought a silver spoon in her chosen pattern. I had been careful to inquire of her mother what her pattern was and where she was registered. Since I was new at this, I had followed my hometown tradition of giving the bride a gift because I was involved in her wedding.

When I returned to school in the fall, I consulted with Claude. When I told him I had never received a check for that wedding, he gave me another word of advice: "Prepare an invoice and send it to the bride's mother." So I wrote a note of apology for being so late in sending my invoice, also asking her whether or not the bride had received my gift of a spoon in her pattern.

Later I received a check for the amount I had charged—not from the mother of the bride, but from the new groom. I was appalled to think that a mother of a bride would pass on her expense to a young husband just starting out in life. I never found out whether or not she had received the spoon. It took me a long time before I knew to speak up and mention my fee whenever I was asked to play for weddings or other events. We small-town girls sometimes have a lot to learn.

Since that time I have played hundreds of weddings. At Eastminster Presbyterian Church in Indialantic, Florida, there were many Saturdays when the pastor and I were involved in two weddings, and we sometimes had as many as three.

CHAPTER 17

The Perfect Wedding Pastor

FOR SEVERAL YEARS I WORKED with The Reverend Kenneth Shick, Sr., who was a most efficient pastor. He didn't need a wedding consultant to engineer rehearsals, because he was the best. He never conducted a rehearsal that lasted longer than one hour. He knew how to keep everything moving.

But his strongest feature was his ability to help a wavering bride make a decision. When the wedding party was assembled in the front pews, ready to begin, he would start with a prayer. Then as he asked each question of the bride, such as "Do you want to have the congregation stand when you enter?" he would immediately suggest an appropriate answer.

If the bride looked at other people and appeared uncertain, he would say, "Your mother is the cue. She will stand, and then the congregation will know to rise." The bride would nod her head, breathe a sigh of relief, and we could continue. Rev. Shick was a master at taking charge. Within a few minutes, he would have everyone lined up and ready to rehearse.

This was a far cry from one wedding rehearsal I played at another church. That preacher did not take charge, and every question he asked prompted a full discussion among the entire wedding party. The rehearsal took about three hours. My "Perfect Wedding Pastor" could have wrapped up that rehearsal within one hour, even allowing time to practice the procession and recession twice. What a blessing Rev. Shick's rehearsals were for us all—especially for the wedding party, who usually had a reservation for a spectacular rehearsal dinner.

CHAPTER 18

Language Barrier

EVEN THOUGH IT'S DIFFICULT to understand someone who murmurs or mutters during a wedding ceremony, that problem is nothing compared to handling a wedding service conducted in a language different from the organist's own.

A young Korean couple conferred with me to plan their wedding music. No problem there—they had both been raised in America. We discussed their favorites, and they made excellent choices for the prelude as well as the marches.

They explained, "We're members of the Korean Presbyterian Church. We asked to be married here (another Presbyterian church) because this sanctuary's size can accommodate the large group of people who will attend. Our pastor will officiate."

I attended the rehearsal the night before the wedding and met the gracious pastor of their church. The wedding would be in Korean. The pastor and I worked out signals so I would get the cues right for the entrance of the wedding party. The bride was radiant, a lovely young woman. Her groom was the gallant gentleman any woman would admire. Their attendants were friends who were very proud to be part of their special day. The final and lovely addition—two petite, adorable Korean children—were the flower girl and the ring bearer. *Why, they are hardly bigger than three-year-olds, and they are handling their parts beautifully*, I thought.

The wedding day dawned. Everything was perfect. My prelude music went well. The pastor signaled me that the mothers were ready to be seated. Beginning their special music, I could see them clearly as they each came down the aisle to their pews. *Good. All is well.*

I began the first wedding march for the attendants. I heard a satisfied stir in the congregation as they caught sight of the lovely bridesmaids floating down the aisle in their traditional dresses. The groom and his attendants awaited them.

Now came my triumphant fanfare for the bride, followed by her theme march. The pastor turned toward me with a big happy smile but shook his head to indicate "No." My puzzled look must have shown on my face as I continued playing the bridal march. He continued his smile as he bent low toward the aisle as if taking care of something there. Suddenly, I noticed movement. Coming toward him, just past the maid of honor in the center, were the tiny children. I hadn't seen them. Realizing my error, I shifted into the soft ending of the number I had just finished. The pastor positioned each child and gave me a nod, smiling broadly all the time. Now: fanfare time.

The rest of the procession went well, including the second fanfare—this time according to plan—and entrance of the beautiful bride in traditional Korean garb. I listened to the vows repeated in their language and received the cue to play the music while they lit their unity candle.

As the ceremony finished, the Korean blessing was spoken and the couple was presented to the congregation. I began the recessional march for them right on cue. Hallelujah!

CHAPTER 19

Wedding Consultants I Have Known

The Carefree Consultant

I WORKED FOR MANY YEARS with an easy-going, happy-go-lucky soul who took life as it came. If a wedding didn't go well, she never used it as an opportunity to learn and improve next time. Her usual response would be, "Well, they're married now. Years from now they'll laugh about that. The main thing is—it's done."

I was able to convince her that I needed a better signal from the back of the church than a wave from her when the wedding party was ready. I told her, "I might mistake that for the hand of someone waving to a friend."

Concentrating on the music I was playing, I only had split seconds to look her way every couple of minutes. So, even though she disagreed, she finally began giving me my preferred signal, using a bulletin to make a large rainbow arc in slow motion. I think doing so made her feel self-conscious. Maybe she was afraid all those people seated with their backs to her were staring at her.

The Ultimate Wedding Consultant

I only encountered her once but would have loved to have worked with her on other occasions. She had a list of the time schedule for the wedding day that would have rivaled a Bill Gates computer program.

One of the instructions fascinated me. It directed the ushers to use a mirror to check their teeth precisely fifteen minutes before their duties began. She had even supplied the mirror. She also brought them sub sandwiches and requested they make sure no lettuce was stuck between their teeth when they walked out to meet the public.

When the appointed time arrived, she, of course, was startled when her ushers were nowhere to be seen. She found them in the parking lot listening to their college's football game. I'm sure they thought it inconsiderate of the bride to plan her wedding on the day of the big game. We were fortunate that the groom wasn't out there, too. In any case, someone shooed them back inside, and the wedding went off as planned.

The Inexperienced Wedding Consultant

I was organist for three of my children's weddings. On the occasion of our younger daughter's wedding I was also, of course, the mother of the bride. She and I had worked out the music sequence with the sound technician. When my son came to the organ to escort me to my pew, the sound technician was to begin playing music over the sound system just as I stopped playing the prelude on the organ.

We thought everything had been worked out properly, but we hadn't planned on an inexperienced wedding consultant. Ours was her first wedding. One of her duties was to send each usher to bring in the grandmothers and mothers. As the mother of the bride, I was looking forward to the honor of being ushered to my pew as the last person before my daughter came down the aisle on her father's arm.

I was playing the music, waiting for the mother of the groom to walk down the aisle, after which my turn would come. I was startled when my son approached me.

As I continued playing, I protested, "Tom, it's not my turn yet. It's the time for his mother." I continued to play.

Tom gave me a smile: "She sent me up here, Mom. Come on."

I kept playing.

"Tom, I'm supposed to be the last one."

Tom, always the charmer, gave me his best smile, held out his arm, and said in his sweetest tone, "You look beautiful, Mom. Let's go."

I admit it—I was charmed. I stopped playing, stepped down, and allowed him to escort me to my pew as the recorded music began. I almost cried as the mother of the groom was ushered down the aisle in my honored place just before the bride.

Maybe I should have taken a cue from my carefree consultant friend: "The main thing is—it's done."

CHAPTER 20

Fascinating Grooms

The Take-Charge Guy

THE MINISTERS AND I usually encountered grooms who were satisfied to allow the bride and her mother to make all wedding-related decisions. But on one occasion, we met a different kind of groom. I learned later that this outgoing gentleman was a manager at Walt Disney World and directed various shows and events. As soon as he came in the door, we knew we had a dynamic leader—whether or not we wanted one.

The bride stood meekly by and watched him direct every member of the wedding party to the spot he designated. The minister asked the bride questions that required a choice: "Do you want to have a kneeling bench?" "Where do you prefer to place the unity candle?" The bride would turn to look at the groom, and he would answer the question. It was fascinating to watch.

To this day, I wonder if they conducted their marriage in that fashion, or if she made some decisions along the way. Of course, it's possible that this was his final opportunity to make decisions as they joyfully began their new life together.

The Rambunctious Guy

Another groom we met showed his pizzazz on the wedding day. On the night of the rehearsal, he proved to be a charismatic, charming person who could joke around and keep everyone happy. His presence energized the entire wedding party, and the bride was a lovely, outgoing person as well.

The day of the wedding arrived. I played the prelude music and then began the march for the groom and groomsmen to enter. The groom came triumphantly through the door, dressed to the hilt in a beautiful white tuxedo. But his accessories were the ultimate: a white top hat and a cane, which he flourished with gusto. What an entrance! The entire congregation broke into applause—quite a beginning to a beautiful wedding.

CHAPTER 21

Fiascoes and Other Fun

Flowers, Anyone?

O H, N O." T HE LADY who placed the flowers in the church
was distressed. That Sunday morning, she discovered
she had to dash to someone's house before the service to get
flowers from their garden.

"Look at this," she said, showing me a bouquet of stems. It
seemed that the men who were in the wedding party the day before had decided to cut off every flower from the Sunday bouquet
waiting in their dressing room. They were already wearing bou-
tonnieres, so we couldn't understand why they had touched the
altar flowers. This was one of several strange situations we encountered when non-members (who may or may not have been
churchgoers) rented the church for a wedding.

The "Experienced" Usher

During one wedding rehearsal, an usher proclaimed with gusto that he had been an usher at several weddings and was very
experienced. An usher is expected to offer his arm to a lady
guest. She takes his arm, and her escort follows behind the two
of them as the usher walks her up the aisle to an available seat.

All went well at rehearsal night, but during the wedding,
I looked up from the organ only to see him walk ahead of a

couple and gesture toward the pew to be seated. I decided his ushering experience came from time spent at a movie theater, flashlight in hand.

The Wrong Pew

Sometimes mixed-up families were involved in the weddings I played. In one of these, the groom's parents had divorced, and each had married another person. This created an interesting scenario.

All participants came to the rehearsal except the groom's father and his wife. It's not unusual for family members who aren't involved in the ceremony to opt out of the rehearsal. Sometimes, they aren't invited. Whatever the reason, these two hadn't rehearsed, so they had no idea where they were to be seated. During the rehearsal, another couple stood in for them, and the usher had practiced seating them.

At the proper time on the day of the wedding, the usher did his duty. He brought the couple who had missed the rehearsal to the second pew on the groom's side. The first pew is always reserved for the groom's mother.

As I started the special music for the seating of the family, I heard murmuring and then loud talk. The sound came from the direction of the groom's father's pew. Meanwhile, the step-mother of the bride had been ushered in and seated across the aisle—also on a second pew. The first pew on that side was re-served for the bride's mother and her husband.

The mumbling and grumbling continued.

Just as the groom's mother was being ushered in, the groom's father stood up, took his wife's arm, and strode forward to sit in the center of the pew in front of them, the one designated for his former wife. He looked angry.

This proved quite a shock for the groom's mother, who was being ushered down the aisle with her husband following. When she saw her ex-husband and his wife seated in her own special pew, she almost had what we Southerners refer to as a conniption fit.

Being a proper lady, she kept her composure and allowed herself to be seated in her honored place in the front pew with her husband beside her. She remained stoic and silent but kept a steely look in her eyes throughout the service.

I commend this lady for choosing not to use her beautiful wedding purse to hit the scoundrel over his head.

How Hot Can It Get?

"Joanna, the bride wants to speak to you." Friends and relatives of the bride and groom were already beginning to arrive at the door of the chapel. I was seated at the organ, preparing to begin the prelude music for the wedding. But one of the ushers approached me as I was putting my music on the organ rack.

The chapel was the perfect size for this small wedding. The bride waited for me at the only entrance at the back. I hurried down the aisle to greet her. We had established a friendly relationship when we planned her music.

There she was, enchanting in her ivory wedding gown with flowers in her hair. But—perspiring! I worried about her make-up, which was flawless.

"How are you? You look beautiful!"

Her expression revealed deep pain. "Joanna, it's too hot in here." She dabbed her upper lip with a tissue. "Can't someone turn up the air conditioner?" It didn't help that she was what my mother would have called "pleasingly plump."

I had to confess: "The air conditioner broke down yesterday afternoon." I hastened to add, "But don't worry. Someone's coming over right now and will fix it."

Her face and posture relaxed, and she managed a weak "OK."

"This will be a gorgeous wedding. You're a beautiful bride."

She managed a smile, and I hurried back to the organ as she went to a side room to await her big moment.

As I played, I thanked God she did not have time to realize that when the repairman came, the job would take him a while. She and the entire wedding party and guests would be well on their way to the reception at another site before we felt the results of his work. But the show must go on.

The Special Wedding Guest

I had just finished playing for a wedding. The bride was lovely. The groom was handsome. All the wedding party were gloriously attired. Everyone followed the script, and the entire ceremony came off beautifully.

I began the recessional march after the pastor's benediction. The bride and groom took their exit down the center aisle, followed by the rest of the wedding party. After they had reached the narthex of the church, one of the ushers turned and came back for the mother of the bride. Everyone was all smiles as he ushered her out, her husband following.

The groom's family was waiting for his mother to be ushered out when they all began chuckling. They began laughing out loud, and soon the entire congregation joined them. From my location, I couldn't see the focus of their attention but continued to play while craning my neck to see.

The pastor was still standing in the center at the front, and he was smiling as well. He said, "As you can see, we have a church cat. The side door was open and she has decided to come in, grace us with her presence, and smell the flowers."

I finally spotted the action and watched as the church cat sniffed each of the floral arrangements in the front of the church. When she had finished her inventory and indicated her approval, she walked out the opposite door in regal style. The audience, smiling as they left, appreciated this perfect ending to a beautiful ceremony.

V. HE GIVETH MORE GRACE:
EXPERIENCES AND EVENTS

CHAPTER 22
Beyond the Sanctuary

ALTHOUGH I WORKED AS a church organist, I also enjoyed playing at other events in the community.

On occasion, I received a call to play for a rehearsal. The organist for an upcoming performance (perhaps Handel's *Messiah* or another production) had to miss a practice session. Then the director called me to come and play for that evening's rehearsal.

In Melbourne our local theater group presented many light operas. I played the organ, and one of my friends played the piano. We accompanied shows such as *The Pirates of Penzance, The Merry Widow, The King and I,* and others. The shows were labors of love for all involved.

Playing for the light opera sometimes became complicated when we traveled to other communities to perform. On one occasion, we arrived at a nearby town about three hours before the performance was to begin. Cast and crew were ready to present Sigmund Romberg's *The New Moon.* I had an hour to acquaint myself with the organ at their civic center. I was in for a shock. The Thomas "organ" consisted of one short keyboard; several keys in the center were gray. I discovered the gray keys were dual-purpose, to be used as solo sounds (louder) or as accompaniment (softer). During the song, the organist had to decide when to push a special button to switch from one volume to the other. What if I switched at the wrong time? I would either overpower the singer or make the music too soft.

Helpless, I asked the director, "What can I do with this?"

He answered, "The best you can."

So that's what I did, with glitches here and there. At one point I was playing a leading solo line to support a soloist. The song "Lover, Come Back to Me" was going well when the melody I was playing dropped out of the gray solo area and into the soft accompaniment mode. But the singer needed that support. He gave me a desperate look as he continued. I knew he was thinking, *Music, come back to me.* He carried on without my strong support until I pressed the special button and reoriented my fingers to the needed part of the keyboard. I doubt if the audience was aware of the problem, but it kept me on edge. After the show was over, I could finally relax.

In addition to playing for musicals, I taught piano in my home and organ lessons at my church as well as in the homes of various students. This required a lot of traveling around the county, but I thought it best for them to learn on their own instruments.

I've found it fulfilling to have several different avenues for my skills as a musician. The position of church organist was my job, but I enjoyed musical theater and training new musicians as well.

CHAPTER 23

The Substitute Organist

Different Denominations

AFTER MY RETIREMENT FROM my final church position, I began to substitute on occasion for my organist friends.

Adapting to different forms of worship in various denominations presented one of the challenges for me as a substitute (or supply) organist. Effective substituting requires familiarity with each type of worship. Preparing for a Methodist or Presbyterian service is simpler than for a more liturgical one. The latter require knowledge of the various responses and chants that make up an integral part. As I gained experience with each denomination, working within the different styles became easier, and changing from one to another became as simple as putting on a different set of shoes.

Just as every organ is different, I encountered different personality types when working with various priests and pastors. One may be completely businesslike, simply expecting the job to be done. He walks in, does his part, and finishes up with little or no interaction with me as the substitute organist. Another pastor may call ahead and point out specific parts of the service that he expects me to handle in a particular way, and still another may meet with me before the service to answer questions.

I learned some important lessons while substituting. Always check with the regular organist, music director, or the pastor to find out if the church prefers a meditative or a robust prelude piece. Always ask many questions about the form of communion service in that particular church (e.g., how often does the pastor speak during the serving of the elements). In some churches, I would play quiet music during communion. In others, the pastor might speak out a verse of scripture now and again. I would need to be ready to bring the organ volume down low as he spoke.

On one occasion, I was asked to play for an evening service at an Episcopal church. This experience was typical of the reception I usually enjoyed. I knew the priest and his wife because she sang in the choir at the church where I was an associate organist. They are loving and friendly people—a joy to know. The priest greeted me with a happy smile and thanked me for being there. The service was for their Spanish congregation, which met on Sunday evenings. Even though I knew the music for the hymns and responses, I did not know where we were in the service. The only Spanish words I know are *si* and *uno, dos, tres, cuatro, cinco.*

The priest's wife sat beside me at the organ, situated in the back of the sanctuary. She pointed to the right place in the service, singing along in Spanish. We both enjoyed it and giggled whenever I gave her a surprised or questioning look. Her big smile told me I was doing a great job. I accepted her evaluation because the congregation sang along heartily, and we all started and ended together. If the proof is in the pudding, then I think even my Spanish pudding turned out well.

Atmosphere and Ambience

I was substituting as organist for a wedding at a church where I hadn't played before. As was my custom, I drove the fifteen or so miles a couple of times that week to practice on their organ. My husband went with me, and we stayed two or three hours each time so I could familiarize myself with the organ and be well-prepared for the pieces I would play.

On the wedding day, I arrived early to set up. People began coming in long before the wedding and talked as they waited together.

As I began to play, I expected them to quiet down, but was I surprised. The members of the wedding party had gathered in the narthex behind me and were loudly enjoying one another's company just as if they were at a big party—which, of course, to a certain extent, they were. I was accustomed to groups who entered quietly and spoke softly before a service began.

I tried increasing the volume of the organ to see if they would realize it was almost time for the ceremony. At that point I thought, *Wow! I could have skipped the hours I prepared* earlier and just walked in today, put flutes on one manual, a different sound on another, hands on the keys, and let 'er rip!

But that's okay. When something like this happens, the organist simply plays for God and for personal enjoyment (and also for that lone person in the group who happens to be listening to the organ). These experiences have helped me realize that the wedding isn't my event but the big moment for the bride, groom, and their guests.

Everybody quieted down for the wedding march, and the service began. Later, during communion, a soloist played a guitar and sang a country song while the congregation listened in rapt attention. I was content to see their reverent attitude once the formalities began.

Choosing a Prelude

The wishes of each congregation are paramount when I play the organ for different churches, so I must follow specific guidelines.

My greatest desire is to blend in so well the minister and the congregation will not miss their regular organist. That would disrupt the worship. I am not there to play showy music that would be appropriate for a recital.

One of the primary parts of the service is the prelude. Each church has its own way of beginning the service. They may prefer a worshipful quiet time as the congregation enters or, in contrast, joyous greetings may make up a vital part of their fellowship. In other words, they may be loud talkers.

I need to make sure I get information from the choir director, the regular organist, and/or the minister about the type of prelude the church prefers. Most use a number that helps bring the congregation into a quiet, meditative, and prayerful attitude. A few others prefer a piece that fosters a feeling of joy and praise.

As with most parts of the worship service, timing is critical. If the spoken word or a procession begins at the listed time of the service, I gauge the playing of my prelude to end at the time set for the service to begin. Sometimes a quiet number is scheduled after the minister or a lay leader has welcomed the congregation. For the former I can choose longer pieces, but for the latter, I need only two minutes or less of quiet music.

Some congregations come in the door with enthusiastic greetings. I need a louder prelude for them so those who enjoy it can hear the music over the voices. For that situation, an exciting interpretation of a praise chorus or hymn is appropriate. Of course, I must admit that I would like someone to hear it besides just God and me.

I keep a folder for each church I serve as substitute organist. In it, I save notes with key contact information as well as the bulletins from each service. When I choose music, I can consult the folder and not repeat a number I've played within the last three years. I use that procedure for offertories and postludes as well. I continue to explore new pieces and learn them well enough to be included in a service so I have a good variety ready at any time.

I want to present the setting and mood of the service in a beautiful way that glorifies the Lord. That fulfills the purpose of the prelude.

Ding-Dong

Almost everyone loves the sound of chimes. Many organs are equipped with a stop named "Chime" or "Carillon." It's an important stop to include when a congregation is choosing an organ for its sanctuary. How lovely to hear the chimes—especially at Christmas.

"Let's include the chimes at the beginning of our eleven o'clock service each Sunday," someone on the music committee may say. They're concerned about that—particularly since they chose to spend the extra money for the chime when the organ was selected.

With the proper approval, chimes then become the standard beginning of the service in their church every Sunday morning.

As a substitute organist, I ask, "How do you use the chime? Do you strike the hour?"

Churches vary greatly in the use of the chime. In one, I was asked to play the Westminster Chimes at the time of the service after my prelude. That's a lovely four-line tune played from the tower of the Westminster Cathedral in London, a very popular bit of music. Grandfather clocks and other clocks often play it, too. When played by clocks, the first line is played at fifteen minutes after the hour, two lines at the thirty-minute mark, three at the forty-five-minute one, and then the entire four lines on the hour, followed by the number of chimes rung to indicate the hour of the day.

There are several variations on the use of the Westminster. In one church I was told, "After you play the Westminster Chimes, strike three notes."

Another church did not use the Westminster. My instructions: "Strike the hour at 11:00 a.m. to signal the beginning of the service."

I played regularly at one church where that was the procedure. I waited until the choir entered the choir loft and then struck the hour. It seemed a bit strange to strike it when the choir arrived about three to five minutes late, but that was the way it went. So I would continue with the prelude until they arrived and then strike the chime eleven times, even though the actual time might be 11:05.

When I went out of town one weekend, an organist friend subbed for me. I had told him about striking the hour on the chime, so he was prepared for that. The next Sunday, a choir member complained, "He rang the chimes before we ever got there, and we were surprised when he started the first hymn." They were offended that he hadn't waited for them to enter the choir loft.

I asked my friend about it. He said, "Well, I kept a check on the clock. When it was eleven o'clock, I sounded eleven times for the time of day and then finished my prelude." That certainly made sense, and I agreed that he had done well. Of course, I also chuckled to myself because he had reminded the choir of their tardiness.

One of the more interesting situations I encountered took place when I substituted for another organist at a different church. That church began their service at fifteen minutes before the hour, at the forty-five-minute mark. I was instructed to play only three parts of the Westminster Chimes, just as it is played on any clock at forty-five minutes past the hour. The only problem? It sounds unfinished, rather like . . .

CHAPTER 24

Unexpected Happenings at the Keyboard

An Unusual Interruption

ONE SUNDAY MORNING, I sat at the piano, ready for the early service to begin. In this church, the piano stood near the pulpit on the floor level. During the first part of the service, someone had shouted a word or two a couple of times, a surprising event in a sedate Presbyterian service. Although startled, I dismissed it, and everything went on as usual.

The minister announced the children's sermon and invited the children to come forward. I played "Jesus Loves Me" as they gathered with him on the steps to the pulpit area. He had just begun the story when I became aware of a presence to my right. There, between the front row of worshipers and me, stood a short, stocky young woman who appeared to be in her thirties.

The people nearby were looking at her and seemed disturbed. No wonder, because she was standing still and staring straight at the minister and the children. It was disconcerting at the least. Everything seemed at a pause.

I decided to repeat "Jesus Loves Me," playing and singing it as well as nodding to the choir to join in. At first they did not get the signal, but as I smiled and nodded to the people in the front row, they began to sing with me. Then the choir and the congregation began.

An usher came forward at that point and spoke softly to the young woman. She allowed him to take her by the hand and lead her to the back of the church. The service continued.

I learned later that she was a mentally ill young woman who lived nearby. Occasionally she wandered away from her mother and would come over to the church. Some members of the staff were familiar with the situation, and they had called her mother to come pick her up. I was relieved to discover she was harmless and thankful for a safe and peaceful ending to a scary few moments.

Illness at Church

A church organist has to be ready for the occasional unusual event that may happen during a service. At one church where I served, the choir and organ were located in a gallery far above the pulpit where the pastor stood. All we could see from that location was the back row of pews. One Sunday, we were in the middle of the service when the pastor stopped and did not go on to the next part. The choir and I could only hear the soft sounds of murmuring voices near the front row of seats below us.

We had no idea what was happening—only that the faces of the congregation in the back of the church showed concern. So I began playing soft music.

After several minutes, the preacher spoke. I let the music slowly fade. He explained, "Someone in the front row has become ill, and the ushers have helped him out to get medical help." After my impromptu solo, we went on with the service as planned.

Power Play

On occasion a storm came along during a church service. Sometimes they passed by with no ill effects, but here in

Florida, an organist must remain vigilant. After all, Central Florida is the lightning capital of the world.

At one church, I was playing on a very old Baldwin electronic organ that could be knocked out of commission when storms were around. I had to remain alert. If I heard a huge crash of thunder and the electricity went off, I hit the organ's power switch to turn it off. Then after the lights in the church came back on, I would turn the organ on again. That would keep it from damage from the burst of electricity.

I've experienced times when the electricity went off suddenly and the church remained without lights or organ. That's when I would grab my music and hurry over to the piano to continue. Sometimes I had to finish the service there. On other occasions, the lights would come back on and I could return to the organ. Exciting times!

Young at Heart

I enjoy working with young people. Once, a choir director and I decided to help one young man after choir practice. He never could sing the right note, so he agreed to stay later so we could work with him.

We tried playing a line of the song for him, but he couldn't sing it. In fact, we weren't quite sure which note he was trying to sing. Everyone has heard of "Johnny One Note." This young man was "Johnny No Note." We reduced our session to the playing of one note on the organ and having him attempt to sing it. When that didn't work, we tried another note. Finally—success! We discovered a note he could match, and he sang it.

Unfortunately, he had no other notes to give us, but we considered it a victory. After that lengthy session, we congratulated him and sent him on his way. He continued in the choir and the others sang loud enough to drown out his voice.

Later, his mother told us, "Thank you so much for taking the time to help him. I know he doesn't sing well." We were glad we took the time to work with him—once. It kept him interested in singing in the choir and being with his friends.

In my years of accompanying youth choirs, I've worked with quite a few young people. I discovered at one church that several of them were piano students. They weren't far advanced in their studies, but they could read the simpler hymn arrangements. So every Christmas season, I worked with each one to prepare a prelude that was a piano-organ duet. I found some duet books for early and intermediate piano students with organ accompaniment. The students would each play the piano part while I played the organ.

The young people enjoyed playing the piano for church and were successful in their endeavors. One of the girls, however, was interested in playing the organ, so I used a duet that had a simple organ arrangement. On that number, she played the organ, and I was the pianist. I scheduled a piano/organ duet as a prelude for each Sunday leading up to Christmas, utilizing the young people of the church.

These students were usually very nervous. We always prayed together before the service and asked the Lord to help us play well and present the message of the song so it would be a worshipful time for the congregation. I also gave them this bit of advice: "If you have any place in the music that gives you trouble while we're playing it, just go on, and don't worry about it. Afterward, when someone compliments you about the music, just say 'Thank you.' Now we're just going to go out there and play that piece for God."

It was wonderful to work with the young people and showcase them before their own congregation, the people who loved them. Knowing they would be nervous, I chose pieces that were below their skill levels. That made it easier for them to play for others. The congregation always showed appreciation for their talent. And—of course—their mothers were delighted.

Something New

One year, our choir director decided it would be unique if the choir sang the Christmas program with taped accompaniment. He knew of other choirs who had done so, but for this church, it was a fresh idea. The tape would provide orchestration and a full sound for all the songs. I felt unsure about it, because it's difficult for a choir to be tied to the tempo of a tape. The director would have no way of adding his own interpretation to the music. Also, if I were accompanying from the organ, I could cover for the choir if anything went wrong. There was no hope of that with a recording.

I was happy that the director was trying something new, but I disliked feeling somewhat useless. In the meantime, however, I played for all the practices.

The director decided that during the service, I would only play for a couple of hymns but stand by with a copy of the music, reading along as the songs proceeded. I would not play, but at least I could serve as a standby. I felt pushed aside, but secretly sure that I would be needed—rather in the manner of "Here comes Mighty Mouse to save the day."

The choir practiced diligently for several weeks with my accompaniment and later with the tape. They also worked with a gentleman in the congregation who recorded Sunday morning services. He came to a couple of the rehearsals and played the tape. Everyone felt ready for the big moment.

At last, the long-awaited day arrived.

The ladies of the church had decorated the sanctuary with greens, poinsettias, candles, and whatever other Christmas items they could find. Wonderful pine scent filled the air. The choir was resplendent in their burgundy robes. The ladies had fresh hairdos. The men sported either carefully combed hair or bald pates. The audience arrived full of happy chatter and Christmas smiles. Everyone was cheerful and looking forward to the performance.

Then—the big moment. The director stood and motioned for the choir to rise. He nodded to the gentleman at the recording station and lifted his arms. We waited for the introductory music.

Nothing happened. The choir waited, still as statues. The director waited, his arms in the air. The audience waited, holding their collective breath.

Uh-oh was all I could think.

After a moment the director lowered his arms. The person in charge of playing the tape walked over to the director. He sheepishly confessed, "I accidentally pressed the record button and erased the first part of the tape."

The director turned pale but recovered quickly. He turned to face the congregation with an impish grin.

"We're going to start again. The beginning accompaniment for that song has been erased from the tape."

He smiled again and the congregation chuckled. They loved this guy.

I thought: *Here I come to the rescue. He'll nod to me, and I can provide glorious organ accompaniment.*

But instead he told the choir, "We'll need to find the right place on the tape where the music begins."

I didn't realize until that moment that I was nervous about "jumping in" and playing the entire program. We had not had enough practice with choir and organ together. I was surprised that I felt relieved and found myself thinking, *Good. Just as it should be.* Even though I had wanted to play, I was pleased that we didn't have to change plans. The choir could go on as usual and not feel uncertain.

He motioned to begin. The tape started with no sound at first. I looked at the score. The part of the tape where the music still existed began halfway down the first page. The choir director began directing and singing at that point. The choir joined in.

The rest of the Christmas program went well. I read along in my score as they sang with the tape. I felt they were to be commended for their diligence and deserved the applause. I was proud of them and even glad that I could just relax and follow along as they sang.

We never used accompaniment tapes again.

Zoning Out

Sometimes after preparing and playing for big events at the church, I would reach a trance-like stage by the end of the final service. All the special rehearsals, in addition to working full-time and caring for my family, had exhausted me.

Christmas was one of those times that involved weeks of preparation. We practiced the Christmas cantata, presented in early December. I worked with various soloists and choirs to be ready for Christmas Eve. When I played the organ at Eastminster Presbyterian, we always had a children's service early in the evening on Christmas Eve. That was followed by another service around 9:00 p.m. led by the youth choir. Then at 11:00 p.m. we would have the Christmas Eve service led by the chancel choir. All of those were very special, and the choirs practiced demanding music that was difficult for them as well as for me. That sort of schedule isn't unusual for any church musician.

We always loved the music we prepared and put all our efforts into presenting it well. It was our offering to the Lord and our blessing for the congregation. The choir, director, and I all wore our robes for the services.

After I finished the postlude for the youth service, I went straight to the choir room in my robe for last-minute practice with the choir before the 11:00 p.m. service. Then we went to the choir gallery, and I began the prelude. After we had put forth our greatest efforts for that beautiful service, we reached the end of the day (or night?). At somewhere between 12:15 and 12:30 a.m. on Christmas Day, I walked out of the church almost in a daze and headed down the sidewalk to my car.

Invariably, someone behind me on the sidewalk would call out, "Joanna." I would turn around, holding my music books and my purse. My friend would be laughing. "Do you realize you're still wearing your choir robe?"

Duh. I would chuckle and trudge back into the church. So ended the long process of an organist's Christmas Eve.

VI. TURN YOUR EYES UPON JESUS:
FINAL NOTES

CHAPTER 25

Poise Is Everything

For several years, I had the pleasure of serving as organist at a wonderful United Methodist church with a dwindling congregation and a small but enthusiastic choir. It was easy to love these people, who poured their hearts and souls into the music each Sunday.

At each rehearsal, the choir director worked with the section of three or four men to help them learn their part in the upcoming special number. They practiced their notes with assurance and gusto.

After that, we put the entire choir together to hear all the parts: soprano, alto, and the men. The men then sang the melody without having a clue that they were not singing the part they had just rehearsed.

They were so adorable (I have to say it) that nobody was perturbed. The choir director kept on directing, I kept on playing, and the sopranos and altos kept singing their parts. We smiled at one another, and the men never caught on. Rehearsal after rehearsal, we followed the same routine and enjoyed joking about it later.

The men were oblivious to their surroundings, and on one occasion, this caused an interesting situation.

We were doing a special program and rehearsed one last time an hour before the performance. Once again the choir director—with unfulfilled hope—took the men through their notes. They sang accurately and well. Then the entire choir sang together and as always, the men changed and sang the melody with the sopranos. Oh, well. The director looked at me and managed to avoid shrugging his shoulders and looking helpless.

The director gave special instructions for one of the songs. "Don't forget, folks. This song was written with a repeat of Section B. Remember that, for the sake of time, we aren't going to repeat that section. We'll continue on to Section C without the repeat."

As we were about to leave the choir room, I added, "Now remember. If anyone makes a mistake, nobody is to look at that person or indicate by facial expressions that anything is wrong. Simply stand and look as if everything is perfectly normal." They grinned and agreed. Later, I could not help but believe that the Lord had given me the inspiration to tell them that.

During the program came the moment of truth: we reached the section that was not to be repeated. But one of the men returned to the previous page and began to sing it again.

Adjusting quickly, I began following him with the accompaniment as the director kept directing. The rest of the choir—God bless them—stood with pleasant looks on their faces, waiting for the next part and not singing. The man who made the error never realized he was singing alone. Because he always sang the soprano part anyway, the melody came through. Such a moment! Such choir poise! When he completed his repeat, the rest of the choir started singing their parts again on Section C, and we finished in fine fashion.

The impromptu soloist never knew what happened and thought everything went according to plan. Best of all, the congregation never realized anything was amiss.

Poise is everything!

CHAPTER 26
When in Our Music God Is Glorified

T HE LIFE OF A PART-TIME organist is a busy one—balancing that job with the other activities of his or her life. But how fulfilling! It's satisfying to come to the end of a special program or service and know everything went well, that God was glorified and the people were uplifted in spirit.

Having retired from a regular contract organist job with any specific church, I'm free to substitute for my fellow organists, my wonderful friends and colleagues.

It is a delight to know that I can keep up my organ practice at the retirement towers where we now live. We have a wonderful five-manual pipe organ right here on the top floor in the chapel. I have the privilege of going there to play for pleasure as well as to work ahead on some pieces that will be ready when I need to play here or somewhere else.

My hope is that anyone who reads this book will learn a bit more about the person who works hard preparing to glorify the Lord with them each week. After all, the accompaniment music for their favorite hymns doesn't just flow from the walls.

Perhaps behind a screen or even in full view is that organist who loves to praise the Lord in beautiful music. That person has joys and sorrows, difficulties and easy days, and family or no family, just as any member of the congregation might have.

How exciting it has been to do what I love and find many friends among choir members, congregations, choral groups, and staff people. Joys, sorrows, successes, goofs—whatever. It all adds up to joyful memories and a wonderful life minding my keys and pews.

I've enjoyed living the life of a part-time organist. I've used the talents He has given me to the best of my ability. And I hope to hear from my Savior when the time comes for me – "Well done, thou good and faithful servant."

www.ingramcontent.com/pod-product-compliance
Lightning Source LLC
LaVergne TN
LVHW041232080426
835508LV00011B/1164